Elisha's exclamation! A sermon, occasioned by the death of the Rev. Hugh Evans, M.A. who departed this life, March 28, 1781, in the 69th year of his age. Preached at Broadmead, Bristol, April 8, 1781, ... By Caleb Evans, M.A.

Caleb Evans

ECCO
PRINT EDITIONS

Elisha's exclamation! A sermon, occasioned by the death of the Rev. Hugh Evans, M.A. who departed this life, March 28, 1781, in the 69th year of his age. Preached at Broadmead, Bristol, April 8, 1781, ... By Caleb Evans, M.A.

Evans, Caleb
ESTCID: T001812
Reproduction from British Library

Bristol : printed by W. Pine, sold by Cadell, Mills, Evans, and the other booksellers in Bristol: and by Buckland, Macgowan and Cater, London, [1781?].
48p ; 8°

Eighteenth Century
Collections Online
Print Editions

Gale ECCO Print Editions

Relive history with *Eighteenth Century Collections Online*, now available in print for the independent historian and collector. This series includes the most significant English-language and foreign-language works printed in Great Britain during the eighteenth century, and is organized in seven different subject areas including literature and language; medicine, science, and technology; and religion and philosophy. The collection also includes thousands of important works from the Americas.

The eighteenth century has been called "The Age of Enlightenment." It was a period of rapid advance in print culture and publishing, in world exploration, and in the rapid growth of science and technology – all of which had a profound impact on the political and cultural landscape. At the end of the century the American Revolution, French Revolution and Industrial Revolution, perhaps three of the most significant events in modern history, set in motion developments that eventually dominated world political, economic, and social life.

In a groundbreaking effort, Gale initiated a revolution of its own: digitization of epic proportions to preserve these invaluable works in the largest online archive of its kind. Contributions from major world libraries constitute over 175,000 original printed works. Scanned images of the actual pages, rather than transcriptions, recreate the works *as they first appeared.*

Now for the first time, these high-quality digital scans of original works are available via print-on-demand, making them readily accessible to libraries, students, independent scholars, and readers of all ages.

For our initial release we have created seven robust collections to form one the world's most comprehensive catalogs of 18th century works.

Initial Gale ECCO Print Editions collections include:

History and Geography

Rich in titles on English life and social history, this collection spans the world as it was known to eighteenth-century historians and explorers. Titles include a wealth of travel accounts and diaries, histories of nations from throughout the world, and maps and charts of a world that was still being discovered. Students of the War of American Independence will find fascinating accounts from the British side of conflict.

Social Science
Delve into what it was like to live during the eighteenth century by reading the first-hand accounts of everyday people, including city dwellers and farmers, businessmen and bankers, artisans and merchants, artists and their patrons, politicians and their constituents. Original texts make the American, French, and Industrial revolutions vividly contemporary.

Medicine, Science and Technology
Medical theory and practice of the 1700s developed rapidly, as is evidenced by the extensive collection, which includes descriptions of diseases, their conditions, and treatments. Books on science and technology, agriculture, military technology, natural philosophy, even cookbooks are all contained here.

Literature and Language
Western literary study flows out of eighteenth-century works by Alexander Pope, Daniel Defoe, Henry Fielding, Frances Burney, Denis Diderot, Johann Gottfried Herder, Johann Wolfgang von Goethe, and others. Experience the birth of the modern novel, or compare the development of language using dictionaries and grammar discourses.

Religion and Philosophy
The Age of Enlightenment profoundly enriched religious and philosophical understanding and continues to influence present-day thinking. Works collected here include masterpieces by David Hume, Immanuel Kant, and Jean-Jacques Rousseau, as well as religious sermons and moral debates on the issues of the day, such as the slave trade. The Age of Reason saw conflict between Protestantism and Catholicism transformed into one between faith and logic -- a debate that continues in the twenty-first century.

Law and Reference
This collection reveals the history of English common law and Empire law in a vastly changing world of British expansion. Dominating the legal field is the *Commentaries of the Law of England* by Sir William Blackstone, which first appeared in 1765. Reference works such as almanacs and catalogues continue to educate us by revealing the day-to-day workings of society.

Fine Arts
The eighteenth-century fascination with Greek and Roman antiquity followed the systematic excavation of the ruins at Pompeii and Herculaneum in southern Italy; and after 1750 neoclassical style dominated all artistic fields. The titles here trace developments in mostly English-language works on painting, sculpture, architecture, music, theater, and other disciplines. Instructional works on musical instruments, catalogs of art objects, comic operas, and more are also included.

old books. new life.

The BiblioLife Network

This project was made possible in part by the BiblioLife Network (BLN), a project aimed at addressing some of the huge challenges facing book preservationists around the world. The BLN includes libraries, library networks, archives, subject matter experts, online communities and library service providers. We believe every book ever published should be available as a high-quality print reproduction; printed on-demand anywhere in the world. This insures the ongoing accessibility of the content and helps generate sustainable revenue for the libraries and organizations that work to preserve these important materials.

The following book is in the "public domain" and represents an authentic reproduction of the text as printed by the original publisher. While we have attempted to accurately maintain the integrity of the original work, there are sometimes problems with the original work or the micro-film from which the books were digitized. This can result in minor errors in reproduction. Possible imperfections include missing and blurred pages, poor pictures, markings and other reproduction issues beyond our control. Because this work is culturally important, we have made it available as part of our commitment to protecting, preserving, and promoting the world's literature.

GUIDE TO FOLD-OUTS MAPS and OVERSIZED IMAGES

The book you are reading was digitized from microfilm captured over the past thirty to forty years. Years after the creation of the original microfilm, the book was converted to digital files and made available in an online database.

In an online database, page images do not need to conform to the size restrictions found in a printed book. When converting these images back into a printed bound book, the page sizes are standardized in ways that maintain the detail of the original. For large images, such as fold-out maps, the original page image is split into two or more pages

Guidelines used to determine how to split the page image follows:

Some images are split vertically; large images require vertical and horizontal splits.
For horizontal splits, the content is split left to right.
For vertical splits, the content is split from top to bottom.
For both vertical and horizontal splits, the image is processed from top left to bottom right.

A
SERMON,

Occafioned by the DEATH of

The Rev. HUGH EVANS, M. A.

Who departed this Life, MARCH 28, 1781,

In the 69th Year of his Age.

Preached at BROADMEAD, BRISTOL, *April* 8, 1781,

Publifhed at the Requeft of the Congregation.

By CALEB EVANS, M.A.

Multis ille bonis flebilis occidit
Nulli flebilior, quam mihi !———
Quando ullum invenient parem?

HORACE.

Precious in the Sight of the Lord, is the Death of his Saints.
DAVID,

BRISTOL:

Printed by W. PINE, in WINE-STREET:

Sold by CADELL, MILLS, EVANS, and the other Bookfellers in BRISTOL:
And by BUCKLAND, MACGOWA, and CATER in LONDON.

TO THE

CHURCH AND CONGREGATION THAT MEET FOR

DIVINE WORSHIP IN BROADMEAD, BRISTOL,

THE FOLLOWING SERMON,

AS A HUMBLE MEMORIAL OF THEIR

LATE HONOR'D AND MUCH-LOV'D PASTOR,

IS INSCRIBED,

WITH THE DEEPEST GRATITUDE

FOR THEIR MANY ACTS OF RESPECT, FRIENDSHIP,

AND AFFECTION TO HIS DECEASED PARENT,

THROUGH LIFE AND IN DEATH,

BY THEIR MUCH OBLIGED

AND AFFECTIONATE FRIEND AND SERVANT,

CALEB EVANS.

BRISTOL, *April* 12, 1781.

A

S E R M O N, &c.

UPON this my firſt appearance in this place, ſince the removal of my honored Father and Colleague in the miniſtry; ſurrounded with theſe enſigns of death, and left, as I now am, alone, I know of no words more ſuitable to the ſolemn occaſion, or more expreſſive of the feelings of my own heart, and probably of yours, my honored friends to whom I am once more permitted to ſpeak; than thoſe of the prophet Eliſha upon the tranſlation of his aged Father Elijah, which you have recorded in the

II. Book of Kings, the 2d chapter and the 12th verſe.

MY FATHER, MY FATHER, THE CHARIOT OI ISRAEL, AND THE HORSEMEN THEREOF!

THE character of a Father is a character truly venerable and amiable, awful and yet endearing.

It

It commands refpect and foftens it into love, it awes and yet it cheers, it infpires the heart with ftrength and vigor, and fills it with delight and joy. There is no character fuperior to that of a wife and prudent, a tender and affectionate Father. What cannot, and what will not a Father do, that enters into the endearment of this character and acts agreeably to it, for the children of his bofom that look up to him for fupport, protection and happinefs? Parental affection is a ftrong and fteady flame, which many waters cannot quench nor the floods drown, and little do children think how many and great the obligations they owe to their parents, till they become parents themfelves. The character of a Father, is indeed the character of God himfelf. The higheft character under which he is made known. After this manner, fays our bleffed Lord, pray ye: Our FATHER which art in heaven! And to give us the ftrongeft idea poffible of the divine compaffion, it is compared to that of a Father. Like as a Father pitieth his children, fo the Lord pitieth them that fear him.

Under this character the prophet Elifha, to exprefs the veneration, the gratitude, the love he felt in his heart towards him, fpeaks of the aged and afcending prophet Elijah in the words before us. My Father, my Father! For though he was not

literally

literally his Father, yet he had been a fpiritual Father to him, and was on many accounts entitled to this honorable and endearing appellation and character. It was by the aged and truly venerable Elijah that young Elifha was firft called, and anointed to the prophetic office. See 1 Kings xix. 16. And the Lord faid unto him, that is to Elijah,—" Elifha the fon of Shaphat of Abelmeholah fhalt thou anoint to be prophet in thy room." From this time, which was long before Elijah's tranflation, Elifha became the conftant companion and friend of the venerable prophet Elijah. Having firft taken a refpectful leave of his parents and friends at home, as appears from the laft verfe of the chapter before quoted, he then arofe and went after Elijah and miniftered unto him. Many circumftances of peculiar endearment arofe, there is no doubt, in the courfe of their united labors in the work of the Lord, which tended every day more firmly and tenderly than ever to bind their hearts to one another. And how affecting the account of their final feparation!

" And it came to pafs," we read, verfe the firft, " when the Lord would take up Elijah into heaven by a whirlwind, that Elijah went with Elifha from Gilgal. And Elijah faid unto Elifha, tarry here I pray thee, for the Lord hath fent me

to

to Bethel." Which requeſt might proceed from tenderneſs to his beloved Colleague and intended ſucceſſor, to ſave him from the pangs of that ſeparation which was ſo ſpeedily to take place. But ſuch was the affection of Eliſha for his honored Father Elijah, as he might well call him, that he determined not to leave him, but to abide with him to the laſt moment. And Eliſha therefore ſaid unto him, " As the Lord liveth, and as thy ſoul liveth, I will not leave thee. So they went down to Bethel ," at which place there appears to have been one of the ancient ſchools of the prophets, over which Elijah probably had preſided, and where, as well as at Jericho afterwards mentioned, Eliſha perhaps had been inſtructed by him, as appears highly probable from what follows. For " the ſons of the prophets that were at Bethel, ſee verſe the third, came forth to Eliſha and ſaid unto him, Knoweſt thou that the Lord will take away thy maſter from thy head to day ?" Alluding to the ancient form of giving and receiving inſtruction · Thoſe that were to be inſtructed ſitting at the feet of the Maſter that inſtructed them, as Paul is ſaid to have been brought up at the feet of Gamaliel, ſo that the removal of a Tutor or Inſtructor, who was elevated on a high ſeat above his pupils, might be conſidered as taking away the Maſter from the head of his ſcholars

lars or difciples. ' Elifha," not willing to be dif-
turbed by any unneceffary converfation, and
wholly intent upon his venerable Father and
Mafter who was fo foon to be taken from him,
replies to thefe fons of the prophets, Yea, I know
it, it is revealed to me as well as you, hold you
your peace. And Elijah faid unto him, Elifha,
tarry here I pray thee, for the Lord hath fent me
to Jericho. And he faid, as before, As the Lord
liveth, and as thy foul liveth, I will not leave
thee. So they came to Jericho. And the fons of
the prophets that were at Jericho, came to Elifha
and faid unto him, as thofe at Bethel had done
before, Knoweft thou that the Lord will take thy
Mafter from thy head to day? To which he replies as before, Yea, I know it, hold you your
peace. And Elijah faid unto him, Tarry I pray
thee here, for the Lord hath fent me to Jordan.
And he again faid, As the Lord liveth, and as
thy foul liveth, I will not leave thee." He could
not bear the thought of parting with him before
the time, but was refolved at all events, whilft he
was continued on earth, to continue with him.
" And" accordingly, " they two went on. And
fifty men of the fons of the prophets went and
ftood to view afar off," expecting the event which
foon after took place, " and they ftood by Jordan. And Elijah took his mantle and wrapped it

B   together,

together, and fmote the waters, and they were
divided hither and thither, fo that they two" Elifha and Elijah, " went over on dry ground. And
it came to pafs when they were gone over, that
Elijah," confcious that the time of his departure
was near at hand, " faid unto his beloved fon and
Colleague Elifha, Afk what I fhall do for thee
before I be taken away from thee. And Elifha
faid, (Oh! what could he have faid more proper
and becoming') I pray thee let a double portion
of thy fpirit be upon me!" He was about to be
left alone, no more to enjoy the counfels, the
prayers, and the affiftance of his venerable Father, and he begged therefore that a double portion of his Father's fpirit might defcend upon
him, that fo he might ftill find ftrength equal to
his day, and that grace which would be fufficient
for him. " And he, that is Elijah, faid, Thou
haft afked a hard thing, neverthelefs, if thou fee
me when I am taken from thee, it fhall be fo unto
thee, but if not, it fhall not be fo. And it came
to pafs as they ftill went on and talked, (O how
muft Elifha's heart have burned within him during this laft interview and converfation with his
venerable Father') that behold there appeared a
chariot of fire and horfes of fire. and parted them
both afunder; and Elijah went up by a whirlwind
into heaven." It then follows, " And Elifha faw

it,

it, and he cried, My Father, my Father, the
Chariot of Ifrael, and the Horfemen thereof!"
It is added, " And he faw him no more."

How applicable, in many tender affecting circumftances, this piece of facred hiftory is, to the
awful event which has lately taken place amongft
us, I need not fay. You have, many of you, I
doubt not, made and felt the application already.
Our Friend and Father, He whom we all loved
and honored as a Father, with whom we long enjoyed fweet fociety, and from whofe converfation
and miniftry we have oft derived the pureft pleafure, is gone from us, for ever gone, gone to
Eternity ! We have borne him amidft a weeping
multitude to his grave. The Chariot of Ifrael,
and the horfemen thereof have efcorted his happy
fpirit to the throne of his God and Saviour ! We
fhall fee his face, and hear his well known pleafing
voice, on earth, no more ! Are we not then ready
to join in the exclamation of the prophet, and
with tears of grief and mingled joy, to cry out as
he did, My Father, my Father, the Chariot of
Ifrael, and the horfemen thereof !

But what is implied in this pathetic exclamation?

May it not be confidered in the

(1.) place, As the language of furprize and confternation ?

Though

Though the event of Elijah's tranflation had been expected for fome time, and it is evident from what paffed betwixt Elifha and the fons of the prophets at Bethel and at Jericho, that it was expected even that day, yet there is no doubt but Elifha was greatly furprized and alarmed when it took place. The fudden appearance of a Meteor in the form of a Chariot of fire and horfes of fire, the feparation that was then inftantly made betwixt him and his dear Father with whom he had been conveifing juft before, and the thought that he fhould now fee him no more, could not but occafion a confiderable degree of furprize and confternation, under the influence of which he might very naturally cry out as he did, My Father, my Father!

There is fomething fo awful in the final feparation of thofe from us whom we loved and honored, and efpecially of thofe with whom we had long affociated with mutual endearment and fatisfaction, that it is impoffible to avoid being furprized and fhocked at it, however long we might have expected it, and how much reafon foever there might be, to be reconciled to it. Elijah had the diftinguifhed honor of being tranflated to heaven without dying, and yet when the moment of his departure came, Elifha his friend and companion, could not preferve an entire compofure

of

of mind, but was in a manner conftrained to give
vent to his paffions in the fudden exclamation before us. How much more then, may we fuppofe
this to be unavoidable, when a friend a Father is
removed from us by Death ! What though we
may have long beheld the fymptoms of decay, and
obferved, with aching hearts, the melancholy pre-
fages of approaching diffolution ; yet ftill, when
the final moment of feparation comes, when the
quivering pulfe beats no more, the clay cold
hands hang down to move no more, the eyes are
forever clos'd, and the fhortening breath at length
ftops and is heard no more. Who can refrain,—
who that beholds, as many of us now prefent
lately beheld, a beloved Parent in fuch circumftances, can refrain from crying out with furprize
and confternation, My Father, my Father !

(2.) This exclamation may be further confidered
as the language of grief and lamentation.

It was not merely the pang of a moment Elifha
felt, when his aged father was removed from him,
but his grief was deep and pungent, and forrow
had filled his heart. He rent his cloaths, we
read, expreffive, according to the cuftom of that
age, of the inward grief and anguifh of his fpirit.
And who could help grieving upon fo trying an
occafion ! To lofe a father, the guide of his youth,

his

his fpiritual friend and inftructor, with whom he had often taken fweet counfel, and to whom he was bound in a friendfhip warm and indiffoluble as that of David and Jonathan ; to lofe fuch a friend, fuch a father, to lofe an Elijah was an affliction of no common fize, and which could not be felt without the moft painful emotions.

If the great God had intended us to be unfeeling Stoics, he would not have implanted fuch paffions in our natures as he has, nor made our hearts " fo apt to feel." Over a Father's Urn, we need not be afhamed to weep, for over the grave of Lazarus Jefus wept. And who can refrain from tears upon the prefent occafion ? Who can help adopting the pathetic exclamation of Elifha, and crying out with the deepeft grief and lamentation, My Father, my Father !

We have loft a Father. Some of us literally fo. The beft of Fathers. A Father who tenderly loved us, who carefully inftructed us, who in all our diftreffes pitied fympathifed with and felt for us, liberally fupplied all our wants according to the utmoft extent of his ability, and with all the warmth of the ftrongeft parental affection daily prayed for us. But his counfels, his prayers, his tears are now no more. The friendly vifits of a Father, his parental tendernefs, his wife

admonitions,

admonitions, his healing confolations, we fhall enjoy no more. We fhall converfe with him on earth no more. His pleafing Countenance is changed and he is fent away, to return no more? God will not be angry with us, that God who himfelf fuftains the character of a Father, if upon fuch an occafion, and under fuch an affliction, we fmite our pained breafts, and cry out, with a degree of anguifh and diftrefs, My Father, my Father!

And methinks I hear many of this congregation ready to fay, with fympathy and warm affection, Nor are you alone in your forrow He was our father as well as yours, our fpiritual Father and Friend. By his inftrumentality we were begotten again to a lively hope through the gofpel. By him our fouls have been edified and comforted, and oft have we fat under his enlivening refrefhing miniftry with great delight, and found the fruit thereof fweet to our tafte. He was our faithful paftor and friend; and moft fincerely therefore can we mingle our tears with yours, crying out, My Father, my Father!—Is not this the language of his affectionate pupils? Is not this the language of the Minifters and Churches all around him, whofe wants he made his own, whofe intereft lay fo near his heart, whofe caufe was fo dear to him? Is not this the language of the numerous poor, whofe

affectionate

affectionate friend he ever was, and who were readily supplied by his instrumentality ? Is it not the language of the orphans that were rescued from destruction by him, and fed and cloathed by his bounty ? Is it not the general language of all that knew him: are they not ready with one voice to cry out, My Father, my Father ! We have lost our active venerable friend and patron, we have lost our Father !

The loss of truly pious, zealous, laborious and successful ministers of the gospel especially of those who have moved in a large extensive sphere of action, and been rendered eminently useful, cannot but occasion the most poignant grief and sorrow. When the righteous, the excellent of the earth are removed, sad must be the state of things indeed, if those that survive them do not lay it to heart. For though God can raise up others of the same disposition and character, yet when he takes away those whom he had raised up and owned blessed and honored, it cannot but be considered as matter of grief and lamentation. In this light, I am persuaded, you, my friends, all feelingly consider the removal of your late beloved Pastor. Which leads me to add,

(3) The

(3.) The exclamation of the prophet in our text, may be further confidered, as the language of the highest veneration and efteem for his Father's character.

My Father, my Father, the CHARIOT of Ifrael, and the HORSEMAN thereof! As though he had faid, Ah! now my venerable Father is gone, who fo often hath flood in the gap, been a terror to the enemies and a confolation to the friends of Zion, the very ftrength and glory of Ifrael feem to be gone with him! In this fenfe, moft expofitors underftand the words. The ftrength and glory of a warlike people, confifted heretofore, in a great meafure, in their chariots of war, which with long fpears faftened to them they drove furioufly againft thofe that oppofed them, and in their cavalry, by which they were enabled fiercely to charge and refolutely purfue the enemy. The prophet Elifha therefore, compares his afcending Father Elijah to the chariots of Ifrael and the horfemen thereof. He faw before him the appearance of a chariot of fire, and horfes of fire, and when he beheld his Father taken from him, he could not but confider their ftrength and glory, the Chariot of Ifrael and the Horfemen thereof, as departing with him. Thus Joafh fee 2 Kings xiii. 14 wept over Elifha when he was dying, and faid, O my Father, my Father, the Chariot of Ifrael and the Horfemen thereof! In like manner we find David when he wept over Abner, to exprefs his high efteem

and

and affection for him, said to those about him. Know
ye not that there is a great man fallen this day in Israel

At the same time that there is no man upon
earth but has reason to acknowledge, that where-
in he may be raised above others in grace, or gifts,
or usefulness, it is by the grace of God he is what
he is, and he has nothing but what he has received,
and consequently nothing in the least to boast of,
yet it is very evident that the great Sovereign of
the universe, whilst he acts unjustly by none, is
pleased greatly to distinguish some, in many respects, above others. He gives to some one ta
lent only, to others two, to others five, and to
others ten. As one star differeth from another
star in glory, so shall it be, we read, at the resurrection : And if it shall be so at the resurrection,
so it must be in a degree now. In some, gifts
and grace shine much brighter than in others.

And have we not in our deceased Pastor, lost
from the hemisphere of the church and the world,
a star of no inconsiderable degree of glory ? You
will not I am sure my friends, for you knew his
worth and loved and honored him, you will not
accuse me of indecency, or of exceeding the
bounds of truth through the partiality of filial gratitude and affection, if I presume thus publicly to
say, He was a burning and shining light. A light
that shone for many years with distinguished lustre,
and

and spread light and warmth and life, in a most extensive manner, all around him.

It was his honor and happiness to descend from parents, illustrious for their piety and benevolence. Their worldly circumstances were not great, but easy and comfortable, sufficing not only for themselves but to enable them also to assist their necessitous neighbours, as they were ever remarkably ready to do. His grandfather Mr. *Thomas Evans* of the Pentre, Brecknockshire, was the son of a substantial farmer in that country of the same name, and was eminent in his day for gifts and grace. In the time of the commonwealth in the year 1649, he passed an examination before the Triers appointed for that purpose men of probity and discernment, and received from them a most honorable written testimonial, which is now in my possession, of his abilities for the Work of the Ministry, and he was appointed by them to preach in the Parish Church of *Maesmyny*, with a handsome stipend. In this situation he continued till the Restoration, and appears to have been very useful, and highly esteemed by those that knew him, and attended his Ministry. When he was no longer permitted to officiate in the Parish Church, as he could not in conscience comply with the terms of Conformity, he formed a separate Society of the Baptist denomination, agreea-

bly

bly to his own principles, which met for divine worship for many years, in his Father's dwelling house, and of which he continued the faithful and affectionate Pastor to the time of his death, in 1688. He suffered much for conscience sake but was carried through all his difficulties, and at length died in peace. He left behind him several children and his eldest son Mr. *Caleb Evans*, a man of good abilities and of a most amiable disposition and character, succeeded him in the pastoral office, and continued in the faithful discharge of the duties of it, till removed by death in the year 1739. And it is remarkable that as this excellent man had many others of his descendants that proved worthy and useful ministers, so one of his grandsons, Mr. *John Evans* is the worthy pastor of the church that was originally formed by his Grandfather, and my great Grandfather to this day. May he be long continued for great and eminent usefulness!

Mr. HUGH EVANS, my honored Father, and your beloved Pastor, was the youngest son of the above-mentioned Mr. *Caleb Evans*, by his first marriage with Mrs *Hannah Lewis* from Hereford-shire, a woman of good repute and substance in that country, of a most excellent spirit, and greatly esteemed for her good sense, piety and benevolence, by all that knew her. His Father,

foon

foon after the years of childhood, difcovering in him early marks of genius, gave him his choice either to be bred up to bufinefs or to be fent to fchool for education. He chofe the latter and was accordingly placed for fome years under the tuition of the Rev. Mr. *Price*, a worthy diffenting Minifter who at that time kept a boarding fchool of high reputation near *Talgarth* in the county of Brecon, and was diftinguifhed in his day as a found claffical fcholar, and an able Mafter as well as Minifter. Under this gentleman my honored Father was thoroughly grounded in the knowledge of the learned languages, and at the fame time had the diftinguifhed happinefs of being brought effectually to the knowledge of Chrift and his own heart. When abfent from his Father (for his pious Mother died foon after fhe had given him birth,) his prayers and pious counfels, he has often told me, feemed to follow him, nor could he reft till he had reafon to hope that his father's God was alfo his God. And I remember to have heard him fay, that the prayers and converfation of a godly family of his Father's acquaintance, and the preaching of that eminent Servant of God, Mr. Enoch Francis,* whom he occafionally heard, and many fentences from whole fermons and pray-
eis

* The father of Mr *Benjamin Francis*, of *Horfley*, and grand father to Mr. *Enoch Francis* of *Frin*.

ers he has often repeated to his family with peculiar pleasure, made such deep impressions upon his mind, as through grace were never obliterated. Soon after this, having occasion to come to this city, to visit a near relation and receive advice for a complaint in his foot, he pursued his learning, if I mistake not for some years, under the direction of the Rev. Mr. *Bernard Foskett*,* at that time the venerable Pastor of this church, and with whom he afterwards served in the ministry, as a son with a Father, with the most perfect mutual harmony and affection, for almost four and twenty years. This primitive christian and truly gospel

---

* This truly excellent man was a bright ornament to his profession and character as a Christian and as a Minister. His funeral sermon was preached by my honored father and his mournful colleague, according to his own express desire, from 1 Cor. 9. 27. *I keep under my body and bring it into subjection, lest that by any means when I have preached to others, I myself should be a cast-away.* Which discourse would have been printed, according to the unanimous request of the congregation, had not the aversion of the author to appear in print, which at that time he never had done, occasioned so long a delay, that it was at length judged adviseable to decline it.

Perhaps it may be some gratification to his still surviving friends, as well as edifying to our younger ministers, to read the following account of his excellent character, which was intended to have accompanied his funeral sermon, but now alas! is annexed to that of its author.

The Rev. Mr. BERNARD FOSKETT was the son of Mr. *William Foskett*, of *North-Crawley* in *Bucks*, a gentleman of good

gofpel Bifhop, foon formed the moft pleafing hopes of the future ufefulnefs of his young pupil, and

repute, eafy fortune, and bleffed with a numerous offspring. He was the younger fon of the family. And, as he early difcovered a tafte for learning, he was put under the care of a very able mafter, with whom he foon made a confiderable progrefs in the feveral branches of literature to which he applied himfelf. Nor was he in the younger part of his life lefs remarkable for ferious and genuine piety for having received the grace of God, we find him at feventeen years of age making a public profeffion of religion. At which time he became a member of the church of Chrift meeting in Little Wild-ftreet, London, then under the care of the Rev. Mr *John Piggott*, now of my worthy and honored friend Dr. *Samuel Stennett* to which fociety he did honor by an upright and exemplary behaviour.

Being thus pioufly difpofed from his youth, and having his mind ftrongly impreffed with the importance of religion, inftead of profe- cuting the honors and profits of the world, which he had a very fair opportunity of doing, he cheerfully devoted himfelf to the fer- vice of the fanctuary And though he had fpent a confiderable time in qualifying himfelf to do good to the bodies of men, he ra- ther chofe now to ferve them in a more important way, by doing good to their fouls ; preferring the character of an able Minifter to that of a fkilful Phyfician. Accordingly, after being regularly in- troduced into the miniftry, he for many years ferved a fmall con- gregation at *Henly-Harding*, in *Warwickfhire*. In which fituation his humane, prudent, and ferious behavior, give him an intereft in the efteem and affection of all who knew him.

But, as this was a fphere of ufefulnefs too confined for a man of his worth, providence foon opened a much larger. In the year 1719, he received a very preffing invitation to the paftoral office in this church, which, not without fome difficulty, he was at length, after a confider- able time prevailed upon to accept And how he has fpent near thirty-

and clearly perceiving that he was poffeffed of the grace of God in truth, encouraged him to devote himfelf

eight years in your fervice, with what honor to himfelf, advantage to you as a church, and reputation to the intereft of Chrift in general, you all know. I might here therefore ftop his works do fufficiently praife him. But I cannot be wholly filent. To fay fomething of fo great and good a man, fo worthy and excellent a Minifter, is a debt of gratitude I owe his memory, and which inclination as well as juftice obliges me to pay.

It is now upwards of twenty eight years fince I had the happinefs of commencing an intimate acquaintance with him, and near twenty four years, fince I have had the honor of ferving with him in the gofpel of Chrift. During this time, it will eafily be imagined, I could not avoid entering into his real character, which was fo truly excellent, that I am in no danger, from the partiality common to friendfhip, of exceeding in my account of it.

His natural abilities were found and good, and his acquired furniture, of which he never affected making a great fhew, was very confiderable. He had a clear underftanding, a penetrating judgement, and a retentive memory. His application to ftudy was conftant and fevere but though he was of a retired and contemplative difpofition, yet he was not fo far detached from the world, as to be wholly unpractifed in the duties of focial life. In the management of his temporal concerns, he was inflexibly juft and honeft; in his counfels, prudent and faithful; in his friendfhips, fincere and fteady, and though he was not a man of ftrong paffions, yet in the relations of a brother and a fon, he was tender and affectionate, dutiful and obedient

His conduct as a chriftian, through a courfe of near fixty years, was moft exemplary and ornamental. So that it may be truly faid of him, he had few equals, hardly any fuperiors. Religion he confidered not as a matter of meer fpeculation, but as an affair the moft facred and important. How ferious and regular he was in his pra

himself to God in the sacred ordinance of baptism, which he accordingly did, with several other young
D persons,

care devotions, in his attendance on family and public worship, and every other religious exercise, they who best knew him will be the readiest to declare. Nor was his religion confined to the closet, the family, or the house of God, but happily diffused its sacred influence through his whole life. Few they were, if any of the christian virtues, that did not shine with a bright and distinguished lustre in his temper and behavior. To delineate them all would carry me too far. I must not however omit to mention what he was always careful to conceal, his disinterested and extensive benevolence; for in this as well as many other respects, in imitation of his divine master, he went about doing good. The necessitous and deserving without distinction partook of his bounty; but the pious poor he ever considered as the special objects of his regard. And while he often judiciously preferred to the indigent sick, he generously supplied them with the means of obtaining what was necessary to their relief. And as the gospel ever held the highest place in his esteem, his charities were chiefly directed in such a manner, as tended most effectually to promote its interests. So that the poor ministers of Christ shared very largely in his compassionate regards, and were multitudes of them refreshed by his liberality. Nor did he confine his benevolence to those of his own sentiments only, but cheerfully extended it to many who differed from him. In a word, as his charities were thus generous and extensive, so the prudence, humanity, and privacy with which they were conducted, secured to him the most cordial respect from those who shared of them, as well as merited the imitation of those who could not avoid knowing them. And as he was thus charitable whilst living, so in this respect as well as many others, being dead he still speaketh.

In the character of a minister, he approved himself judicious, prudent, faithful, and laborious. His religious principles, which were those commonly called *Calvinistical*, he ever maintained with

persons, August the 7th, 1730, the ordinance being administered by Mr. Foskett himself, and a suitable

a steady christian zeal. But though he was strenuous for what he apprehended to be the truth, yet was he fond of no extreme. While he strongly asserted the honors of free grace, he earnestly contended for the necessity of good works, preaching duty as well as privilege, and recommending holiness as the only way to happiness. And with what judgment, seriousness, and affection, he insisted on these important and interesting subjects, you cannot but remember, as also the extraordinary weight, which these his instructions received, from his own very regular and pious example. He was indeed a pattern to the flock in word, in conversation, in charity, in spirit, in faith, in purity. Nor was he without the pleasure of seeing his labors crowned with great and happy success, as sufficiently appears from the present very flourishing state of this Community.

To all which I may add, that in the office of a Tutor he failed not to pursue the same ends, which animated his profession as a Christian, and his public labors as a minister. He was always studious to promote the real advantage of those under his care, endeavouring to lead their minds into a general knowledge of the most beneficial and important branches of literature. And though he judged a superficial education best suited to the years and capacities of some, yet he encouraged and assisted others in the pursuit of a more finished one; conforming himself in the whole to the professed design of the founder of this Institution. And it is remarkable of most of those that were under his care, that they approved themselves truly serious, and do at this time with great reputation fill many of our churches.

In the regular and unwearied discharge of all these several duties of his profession he spent near forty years, during which time he suffered little or no interruption in his work from the disorders incident to human nature. But at length, by a paralytic seizure he

...... Sermon preached upon the occasion by the late excellent and amiable D. *Stennett* He now pursued his studies with redoubled vigour, being desirous of serving God in the gospel of his son, should he be counted faithful and put into the ministry, and, as I have heard testified by many that were well acquainted with him at this time, he was remarkably diligent in business fervent in spirit, serving the Lord, and gave early and striking presages of that future acceptance and success

D 2   with

...... the notice of his approaching dissolution. In these circumstances he continued near a fortnight still enjoying the perfect and undisturbed use of his reasoning powers, and still discovering the same serene, pious, and heavenly spirit, which had ran through his whole life. Within a day or two of his decease he addressed himself to me with a peculiar solemnity, and an uncommon pathos, in these words "I have done with many of the inhabitants of the world, and I have now nothing to rely on, but the merits of my dear Redeemer, who of God is made, I trust, to me, wisdom, righteousness, sanctification, and redemption this is all my salvation and all my desire!" Sustained with these blessed hopes of the everlasting Gospel, he cheerfully submitted to the stroke of death, and quietly fell asleep in Jesus, September 1—, 1758, in the seventy fourth year of his age

Thus liv'd and thus di'd this great and good man. May we not only say, Blessed is that servant whom his Lord when he cometh shall find so doing! Such surely, need not fear being at last cast-away, but may depend upon receiving, through rich grace, as we doubt not our departed friend and Father has, abundant entrance into the everlasting kingdom and glory of their God and Saviour.

with which his divine Master defigned to honor him On the 17th of Auguft 1733, he was called forth by this church to preach the gofpel and foon after received invitations from two of the moft refpectable churches of the Baptift denomination, in London and Southwark,* to pay them a vifit and preach amongft them as a candidate, both of thefe churches being at that time deftitute of paftors When he had fulfilled his engagements with thefe churches, he received an unanimous and affectionate invitation to the paftoral office from each of them And in December the fame year, he received an invitation alfo from this church to become an affiftant to their worthy paftor. Which latter invitation, notwithftanding many difcouraging circumftances at that time, and much fairer profpects as to the world at each of the other places, after ferious deliberation and earneft prayer, he thought it his duty to accept of in the year 1739 he was called to the office of a Teaching Elder, that he might regularly adminifter the ordinances in cafe of the illnefs or abfence of the paftor, and fucceed him immediately upon his death which call he likewife accepted.

*the one meeting in Devonfhire-Square and afterwards under the care of the Rev. Mr Da.. and the other in Unicorn... which had been under the care of the Rev. Mr. Smith,

ed and was soon after ordained to that office, notwithstanding the pressing invitation he at that time received from the Baptist church in Exon. In the year 1750, upon the death of the Rev. Mr *Wilson*, he received an invitation from the Baptist church in Goodman's fields, London, but as the church here were unwilling to part with him, he could by no means think of rending himself from them. Here he began his ministry, here the Lord was pleased eminently to own and honor his ministry and here he closed it. having been a worthy member of this church for more than fifty years, and a faithful, laborious, successful minister and pastor of it for more than forty-seven years.

In the year 1735, he married *Sarah*, the eldest daughter of Mr. *Joseph Browne*, of this city, a woman of uncommon excellencies, and with whom he lived in the most perfect conjugal felicity, till deprived of her by death, whilst on a journey together, at *Pershore* in Worcestershire, in the year 1751. By this marriage he had a numerous offspring; three of whom only survived him, one son, his happy Colleague in the ministry for almost two and twenty years, and now his mournful successor, and two daughters, who will, I trust, long remember and imitate the many virtues of their inestimable parents.

In

in the year 1752, he married his second wife, Mrs. *Ann Ward*, the daughter of Mrs. *Margaret Brain* of this city, and the widow of Mr. *Nathaniel Ward* of London. A woman of real worth and piety, the intimate friend and companion of his former wife, and with whom he lived in a state of great social happiness to the time of her death, Jan. 23, 1776 * Out of ten children by this marriage, five only remain, three sons and two daughters, the children as we all were of many prayers, and who will I trust every one of them, as some of them have already done, in an open and public manner rise up to call their God and the God of their pious parents blessed! That so though we are for a time painfully separated from our dear parents, we may rejoice in hope of meeting them again in heaven to be separated from them no more for ever.

There was something pleasing in the person and appearance of our deceased Pastor and Father. He was of a middling size and stature, enjoyed good health, and his countenance was remarkably open, manly, and engaging, expressive of the soundness of his understanding, and the warmth and benevolence of his heart. Strong masculine good sense, directed by fervent piety and an ardent

dent

* For a further account of each of these worthy women, see a funeral sermon for the latter preached by C. Evans, Jan. 23, 1776.

dent zeal for the glory of God and the happinefs of mankind, all that knew him will, I am confi dent readily acknowledge, were the leading cha- racteriftic features, if I may fo exprefs it, of his expanfive heaven illumin'd mind. His addrefs was eafy, his converfation familiar, cheerful and affectionate Never was his family happier than when he was with them. A better Hufband, a better Father, a kinder Mafter, a more faithful and affectionate friend, furely there could not be ' The generous warmth, the enlivening fpirit of a friend," was never more fully exemplified than in him.

Nor were there many that excelled him as a Tutor. He labored affiduoufly in this character, not merely to form fubftantial fcholars, but as far as in him lay was defirous of being made an inftrument in God's hand of forming them able, evangelical, lively, zealous Minifters of the gofpel. And it was an inexpreffible pleafure to him to fee fo many that had been under his tuition fulfil his expectations concerning them. Not long before his death, whilft he was fitting in the Lecture room with many of his pupils about him, he fpoke with tears of joy to this effect. " I am happy to fee thefe young men rifing up, I hope for great and emi- nent ufefulnefs in the Church of God, when I and many others fha'l be here no more." My

young

young friends, as I know you loved and honored
your deceafed Tutor whilft living, fo I truft it
will be your earneft defire to realize his prophetic
hopes concerning you now he is dead!

But how fhall I defcribe my dear and honored
father in the character of a Minifter and Chriftian
Preacher! His gift in prayer was uncommon
No one I believe ever heard him pray twice
alike, and yet perhaps feldom if ever thought he
could have prayed with greater pertinency pro
priety and pathos than he did, every time he engaged in that folemn duty. In the family from
day to day, at our private occafional meetings,
in the public fervices of the Lord's Day, and
upon extraordinary occafions, there are num-
bers, not only in this Congregation but alfo in
many others where he has occafionally officiated
who will not eafily or foon forget with what variety, copioufnefs, dignity, and unfeigned fervor
he would pour out his Soul to God. He wreftled
with God and prevailed. Prayer was his element,
and he never appeared to enjoy himfelf more than
when engaged in that duty. His prayers evi-
dently flowed from the fulnefs of his heart, and
feemed to breathe the earneft language of the Pa-
triarch, I will not let thee go except thou blefs me.

His pulpit compofitions were clear, nervous and
pathetic Few men were more capable of taking
a large

a large, comprehenſive, maſterly view of a ſub-
ject, or of repreſenting it with greater perſpicuity,
energy and fervor. As he always preached without notes, though he wrote, in his younger days
eſpecially, the ſubſtance of all his ſermons in ſhort
hand, of which he was a compleat maſter; it cannot be ſuppoſed that his diſcourſes always appeared with equal advantage. But I may venture to
ſay they were never mean, often excellent, and
upon ſome occaſions truly great and aſtoniſhing.
His language was maſculine. juſt and ſtrik-
ing, as diſtant from every thing low and puerile
on the one hand, as from every thing pompous
and affected on the other. His voice was clear
and ſtrong, and his delivery perfectly intelligible,
eaſy, graceful, commanding and unaffected. A
more proper decent manly elocution has ſeldom
been the felicity of any man. Nor did any
preacher perhaps ever know better than he did,
eſpecially at ſome happy ſeaſons, what it was *do-
minari in concionibus*, as one expreſſes it; to reign
over his audience, enlightening their underſtand-
ings, convincing their judgments, and then kindl-
ing all their nobleſt paſſions into a blaze of devo-
tion. When he was in the full vigour of his
mental powers, with what admiration have theſe
eyes, in early youth, beheld him; and with what
delight have theſe ears caught the heavenly ſounde

E   tha

that have been uttered by him! O how would he
deſcribe the terrors of the law, and the aſtoniſhing grace of the goſpel! How would he repreſent
the guilt and pollution of ſin, the danger of the
ſinner, and his abſolute need of an intereſt in the
Almighty Savior! How would he expatiate upon
the glories of the perſon and chaiacter of Chriſt,
and the immutability of that glorious, everlaſting
covenant which is eſtabliſhed in him! How
would he lay the ſinner in the very duſt before
the throne of a holy God, and magnify the riches
of free grace in his ſalvation! How would
he deſcribe the beauties of holineſs, and with
what irreſiſtible eloquence inculcate that great
important truth, that without holineſs no man
ſhall ſee the Lord, and that except therefore
a man be born again, he cannot enter the kingdom
of God! How would he diſplay the joys of
heaven, and the torments of hell! The rivers of
pleaſure at God's right hand, and the worm that
never dies, the fire that is never quenched! How
affectionately would he addreſs the young and the
old, the rich and the poor, fulfilling the miniſtry
of reconciliation with which he was entruſted, and
beſeeching them in Chriſt's ſtead to be reconciled
to God! A Boanerges, a ſon of thunder to the
careleſs and ſecure, a Barnabas, a ſon of conſo-
lation to the contrite and afflicted. His religious
ſentiments,

fentiments were perfectly evangelical. The great
leading doctrines of the gospel he steadily and affectionately adhered to through life. He prized
and practically improved them; and knew well,
when neceffary, how ably and earneftly to con-
tend for the faith once delivered to the faints.
But he always did it with a fpirit of love towards
thofe who differed from him, adhering ftrictly and
inviolably to that excellent maxim of his bleffed
Mafter, Judge not that ye be not judged. He
had a truly Catholic heart; a heart too large to
be confined within the narrow limits of party.
He fincerely loved good men of every denomination, and was ever ready cordially to fay,
Grace be with all them that love the Lord Jefus
Chrift in fincerity.

In labors as a minifter, few have been more
abundant. Not only did he labor in feafon and
out of feafon for a long courfe of years in this
congregation, with fcarcely any interruption from
illnefs, excepting the confinement of a few weeks
with a fractured bone, but his labors were extended far and wide all around him. He had the
care of many churches lying upon him, and was
indeed ready to fpend and be fpent. Many and
long were the journies he travelled to affift at the
ordination of his younger brethren, and at our
Annual Affemblies, both in the principality, his

native

native country which he ever loved and honored*, and in different parts of England. And with what dignity, affection and fervor he conducted these solemnities, with what seriousness and energy he would describe the nature and importance

* In his frequent visits to the principality, it was his pride and glory as well as pleasure to be able not only to converse with, but also to preach to his countrymen in their native language. And it is remarkable that the very first sermon he ever printed, was a sermon preached at a WELCH Association, in June 1773, soon after the death of an aged and very worthy minister in that country. The subject was, Zech. i. 5. " Your fatners, where are they ? And the prophets, do they live for ever ?" Having been thus undesignedly led to appear in print, though he had upon many former occasions resisted the most pressing solicitations of a like nature , he was the more easily induced to comply with the wishes of his friends in the publication of two other discourses the same year. The one, entitled " The Able Minister," preached at the Annual Meeting of The Bristol Education Society , and the other at the ordination of the Rev. Mr. T. Dunscombe, at Coate in Oxfordshire, from Phil. ii. 29. " Receive him therefore in the Lord with all gladness, and hold such in reputation " The above three sermons do honor to the abilities of their author and were all he ever published ; and as his very numerous manuscripts are all in a short hand principally of his own, and which cannot be decypher'd, so that it is impossible to recover those many energetic masterly and powerful discourses which still live in the remembrance of those that had the happiness of hearing them, we must be content with this slender memorial of those excellent talents, which rendered the possessor of them so justly dear to us whilst living, and his memory so precious now he is dead.

ance of the ministerial character, and with what
gravity and power he would charge his younger
brethren to take heed to the ministry they had
received in the Lord, to fulfil it, and to let no
man have reason to despise their youth ; with
what divine eloquence he would display the unutterable glories of the gospel, and preach Christ
crucified, to the Jews a stumbling block, and to
the proud Greeks foolishness, but to them that are
saved the wisdom of God and the power of God
unto salvation. With what strength of argument,
and force of language, he would discourse upon
these and other subjects of a like nature upon such
occasions, I need not say ; there are great num-
bers throughout the land ready with pleasure to
declare it. And how cheerfully at these as well
as others seasons did he embrace every opportunity that offered in his going out and returning
home, of spreading the favour of the knowledge
of Christ and salvation by him ! He was not a
slothful servant, but truly active, zealous, laborious and unwearied in the service of his beloved
master. He counted not his very life dear to
him, so that he might finish his course with joy,
and the ministry which he had received of the
Lord Jesus, to testify, wherever he went, the
glorious gospel of the grace of God. Nor did he
labor in vain, or spend his strength for nought,
but

but it pleafed God both at home and abroad, to give him many feals to his miniftry, many that were his joy here, and will be the crown of his rejoicing in the day of the Lord Jefus hereafter.

The gravity and compofure with which he adminiftered the ordinance of baptifm, often in large affemblies, have been remarked by many. There was a dignity and reverence in his manner, that cannot eafily be defcribed. And how often have our hearts burned within us, when we have fat down with him at the table of the Lord, and he has opened his heart in prayer to God for us, and affectionately talked to us of the love of Chrift there! And over the graves of his departed friends, with what folemnity and pathos would he fpeak of death and all its terrors, and then pour into the afflicted hearts of furviving mourners the confolations of the gofpel, by which life and immortality are brought to light, and death is fwallowed up in victory!

Nor can I omit to mention how eminently he was given to hofpitality His houfe, his table, his heart were always open, and it was his delight to do good to all men, efpecially to the houfhold of faith. He was in a manner the Father of the Annual Collection which you have fo generoufly made for many years, for the fupport of Minifters and Churches in the Country: for it was principally

pally by his inftrumentality that it was raifed from a very low ftate indeed to a very confiderable fum. Nor will it be foon forgotten with what copiouf-nefs, variety and perfuafive eloquence he would plead the caufe of his brethren upon thefe occa-fions.

I might mention the peculiar freedom perfpicuity and force with which he would ex-plain and illuftrate the facred fcriptures, without any premeditation, at our private weekly meetings, fo that it might be truly faid of him, as it was of his divine Mafter, He taught as one having au-thority, and not as the Scribes. I might take notice of his truly friendly and affectionate vifits to the fick and afflicted, in all whofe afflictions he was afflicted, efteeming it his honor and his hap-pinefs to be the inftrument of pouring the balm of divine confolation into their wounded hearts. I might mention his fteadinefs impartiality, and zeal, and at the fame time his gentlenefs and for-bearance in the exercife of Chriftian difcipline in the church And his affectionate concern for the peace, the comfortable fupply and profperity of other churches, as well as more immediately of that over which he prefided But it were endlefs to enumerate all the excellencies of that charac-ter which filial affection hath led me to attempt to defcribe, and the remembrance of which I wifh to perpetuate. I have never meant to fay

it

it was faultlefs; but I verily believe it had as few defects and as many virtues in it as in the prefent imperfect ftate can be expected.

But no man could have a lower opinion of himfelf, and of his many labors and exertions in the caufe of Chrift, than he had. Not very long fince, when lamenting his ufeleffnefs, upon his being reminded of his former activity and zeal, he replied, that at the fame time he was thankful he had been enabled to do any thing for fo good a Mafter, yet he was fo far from thinking he had done as much as he ought, that he was ready rather to cry out with dying Grotius, " *Heu, vitam perdidi, operofe nihil agendo!*" Alas, I have thrown away my life in laborious trifling! Though there was never perhaps any man that had lefs reafon than he had to adopt fuch an exclamation.

It is now more than two years at leaft, fince his ufual ftrength and vigour began very vifibly to decline, and for the laft year very rapidly indeed. He was however enabled, after a threatening fit of illnefs and diforder during which he enjoyed much of the prefence of God and the joys of his falvation, to attend the laft Annual Affociation at *Frome*, in the month of June, and to take a folemn leave of his friends and brethren there, in an awful and affecting difcourfe addreffed to hearers, profeffors and minifters, from thefe alarming words,

words, Gal. vi. 7. " Be not deceived, God is not mocked." After his return, he preached two Ser-mons from these words, James i. 22. " Be ye doers of the word, and not hearers only, deceiv-ing your ownselves." And soon after closed his public ministry, though alas ! we then knew it not, with a truly paternal address from these words, Gal. iv. 19. " My little children, of whom I travail in birth again, until Christ be formed in you." A sermon that was blest to many, and I trust will be long and affectionately remembered by us all. In the month of October, if I mistake not, he administered the ordinance of the Lord's Supper, and after that prayed once in public, and so put a period to his long, faithful and affec-tionate services amongst us.

During his declining state, it is scarcely possible for me to describe his placid resignation to the divine will, his meekness, his thankfulness to all around him. Every passion seemed to be extin-guished but that of love. He often admired, and with tears of joy adored the divine goodness to-wards him, and overflowed with good will and af-fection to his family, his friends, and all his connec-tions, expressing the sincerest good-wishes for them, and the warmest gratitude for all their kindness to him. To this church and congrega-tion he was most affectionately united, and your welfare, my honored friends, as individuals and in your social capacity, lay very near his heart. It

was

was a joy almost too great for his feeble frame, to
attend the Lord's Supper with us, as he did for
the last time, in the month of January, when there
was a considerable addition made to our number,
and some of them, O what a mercy! from his
own family. I remember he once said, when
speaking of the prosperous state both of the church
and academy, that he thought he might say with
good old Simeon, " Lord, now lettest thou thy
servant depart in peace, for mine eyes have seen
thy salvation." After this he attended divine
worship once only, and was then confined en-
tirely to his house, soon after to his chamber, and
then to his bed, till at length he gently slept the
sleep of death and after some short conflicts with
nature, during which his senses appear to have
been locked up, quietly breathed out his happy
spirit into the bosom of Jesus his Redeemer and
Savior, to be admitted by him to the nobler worship
of the spirits of just men made perfect in heaven

In the many occasional conversations I had
with him at different times during his state of
weakness, it has often refreshed and supported me
more than I am able to describe, to find him con-
tinually calm, resigned, and truly peaceful and
happy He very frequently repeated with parti-
cular pleasure, the following lines from Dr. Watts.

" O could we die with those that die,
And place us in their stead,
Then would our spirits learn to fly,
And converse with the dead " —

and often used to say, " I blefs God, I am not, through grace, at all afraid to die. I am waiting till my change comes. My flesh and my heart fail, but God is the strength of my heart, and my portion for ever. Nature, said he, fails, and upon its being said to him, But grace cannot, he replied with a pleasing emphasis, " No, no, that never fails." He appears to have been kept in perfect peace to the very last, and to have ended his days on earth, as our honored brother expressed it at his grave,* " like a calm summer's evening without a cloud." He was gathered in as a shock of corn fully ripe, and it was a mercy to him, and a peculiar mercy to us all that he was so gradually, and I had almoft said imperceptibly removed from us. Yet still, who that knew his worth, can reflect upon the death of fuch a man fuch a minifter, fuch a Father, without emotion and concern ? How natural the exclamation of the prophet, as expreffive of the highest efteem and veneration, My Father, my Father, the Chariot of Ifrael and the Horfemen thereof! The beauty of Ifrael is flain, the mighty is fallen !

But bleffed be God we do not forrow as without hope, for if we believe that Jefus died and rofe again, even fo them alfo which fleep in Jefus will God bring with him. And I think it is not at all unnatural to confider the exclamation in our text, in the   (4) And

---

* The Rev. Mr. Tommas, in his very fuitable and pathetic addrefs upon that folemn occafion.

(4.) And laſt place, as expreſſive of a degree of triumph and joy.

At the ſame time the prophet could not but be grieved to part with ſuch a father as Elijah had been to him, yet it muſt have given him joy to think of his honorable and happy tranſlation to a better world. He ſaw a chariot of fire and horſes of fire ſent down from heaven to convey his father thither. And he cries out, My Father, my Father, the Chariot of Iſrael and the Horſemen thereof! Surely there muſt have been a degree of triumph and joy in the exclamation, as well as of the other paſſions which have been already deſcribed. It is as though he had ſaid, Well, though I ſee I muſt part with my dear my much loved Father, who was the very Chariot of Iſrael and the Horſemen thereof, yet behold a chariot of love is ſent down from the heavenly courts to bear him to thoſe bright abodes where there's a fullneſs of joy, and pleaſures for evermore! Let me then catch his falling mantle, and go on my way rejoicing, till the happy moment comes, when there where he is I ſhall be alſo.

And have we not the like conſolations upon the preſent mournful occaſion! Though our dear Father was not removed from us in the extraordinary manner Elijah was, yet hath not the voice from heaven aſſured us, that Bleſſed are the dead who die in the Lord, for they reſt from their labors, and their works do follow them? It is true,

we

⟨ e left the mortal body of our friend and Father
in the grave   but did we leave the immortal fpirit there? No   that is now triumphing around
the facred throne, and is happy in the fociety and
converfe of its kindred immortals, with Abraham
and Ifaac and Jacob, and many pious friends,
and beloved relatives gone to glory before him,
and who are now joyfully worfhipping before the
throne of God and the Lamb together with him!
O with what accents of joy and triumph are they
ready to cry out, " To die is gain ! To depart and
be thus with Chrift is far better than it ever was or
could be with us before ! Our tears are wiped
away, our fins and infirmities have all left us, our
robes are wafhed and made white in the blood of
the Lamb, we have palms of victory in our hands,
and all our work is praife. Nor fhall our bodies always lye in the grave, as they now do, but
the morn will come, (tis a part of our joy to look
forward to it ') the refurection morn will arrive,
when the trumpet fhall found, the graves be opened, and the dead raifed incorruptible. Then
fhall he who once lay in the grave himfelf, he who
is the refurrection and the life, the center of our
faith on earth and the fource of our joys in heaven, then fhall he appear in all his own refplen-
dent glory, and the glory of his Father and the
holy angels, and we fhall appear with him in glory ' Our mortal bodies fhall put on immortality,
be fafhioned like to the glorious body of the fon

of

of God himſelf, and death ſhall be ſwallowed up abſorbed, for ever loſt in compleat everlaſting victory. Then ſhall we ſing with all the redeemed, with tranſport inexpreſſible, O death where is thy ſting, O grave where is thy victory ! The ſting of death is ſin, and the ſtrength of ſin is the law, but thanks be to God who giveth us the victory, through Jeſus Chriſt our Lord ! Then ſhall we enter with all the brilliant throng of the redeemed, through the gates into the heavenly city, there for ever to behold the face of our God and Savior in righteouſneſs, to be changed into his image from glory to glory, and to aſcribe with unutterable delight and joy, bleſſing and honor, thankſgiving and praiſe, to him that ſitteth upon the throne, and to the Lamb that was ſlain to redeem us to God, to him who hath loved us and waſhed us from our ſins in his own blood, and hath made us Kings and Prieſts unto God and his Father for ever and ever !"

At this blisful period, that tranſporting ſentence which you ſo lately heard moſt pathetically deſcribed,* ſhall be, we doubt not, pronounced upon our deceaſed friend and Father: " Well done, good and faithful ſervant, thou haſt been faithful over a few things, I will make thee ruler over many, Enter thou into the joy of the Lord !" This ſentence, may it be our happineſs to hear pronounced, and in all the unutterable bliſs and

glory

† By the Rev. Mr. Francis in his excellent ſermon at the interment from Matt. xxv. 21.

glory included in it, may we, through the riches of divine grace, for ever fhare!

Let us then comfort one another under the prefent afflictive providence, with thefe confolations. Let us be thankful that God ever gave us fuch a Father, fuch a Paftor· And that he continued him fo long to us, and did fo much for and by him Let us imitate the many things we faw in him fo highly worthy of imitation, and honor his memory by imbibing his fpirit and copying his bright example.

And though parents die, and minifters die, let us rejoice that Jefus Chrift the great Head of his church lives, and is the fame yefterday, to day, and for ever. He can pour out a double portion of the fpirit of our afcended Elijahs, upon our furviving Elifhas. In him all fulnefs dwells. And his church and people he will not leave nor forfake, but becaufe he lives, he will moft affuredly take care of and provide for them, and fee to it that they fhall live alfo. Let us look to him, and depend upon him. And let thofe of us that have literally loft our Father, remember that we have not loft our Father's God, but that in him the fatherlefs ftill find mercy, that he is ftill a God hearing prayer, and able to make all grace to abound towards us. May he ever be our truft, our confidence, our portion! And though our beloved Father fhall no more come back to us, may we have this for our confolation, that when

we

we die we shall go to him! And in the last tre-
mendous day, may we all meet him with joy and
not with grief! Meet him in the happy train of his
spiritual children, whom he shall then present to
his divine Master, saying, " Lord, here am I,
and the children thou hast given me!"

But should there be any who have heard the
gospel from his lips, that shall be found at last
despisers of it, where shall they appear! How will
they bear to lift up their guilty heads, when they
shall see him who once affectionately preached the
gospel of life to them, obliged to become a swift
witness against them! God forbid a scene so awful, should ever be realized! But this know, the
faithful ministers of Christ are a sweet savour unto
God in them that perish as well as in them that
believe, and though many may despise them and
their message, yet still the gospel in spite of all the
opposition made to it, shall run and be glorified,
and the redeemer shall see of the travail of his
soul and shall be satisfied. And however his
faithful servants may now be treated by the pro-
phane and ungodly, the illustrious hour is hasten-
ing on and will soon arrive, when they shall shine
as the brightness of the firmament, and as the
stars for ever and ever.

THE END.

CPSIA information can be obtained
at www.ICGtesting.com
Printed in the USA
BVHW081850071118
532428BV00009B/248/P